OUTDOOR SKILLS for KIDS

HELP US KEEP THIS GUIDE UP TO DATE

Every effort has been made by the author and editors to make this guide as accurate and useful as possible. However, many things can change after a guide is published—regulations change, facilities come under new management, and so forth.

We would love to hear from you concerning your experiences with this guide and how you feel it could be improved and kept up to date. While we may not be able to respond to all comments and suggestions, we'll take them to heart, and we'll also make certain to share them with the author. Please send your comments and suggestions to falconeditorial@rowman.com.

Thanks for your input!

OUTDOOR SKILLS for KIDS

The Essential Survival Guide to Increasing Confidence, Safety, and Enjoyment in the Wild

BUCK TILTON • CHRISTINE CONNERS

FALCON®

Essex, Connecticut

FALCON®

An imprint of Globe Pequot, the trade division of
The Rowman & Littlefield Publishing Group, Inc.
4501 Forbes Blvd., Ste. 200
Lanham, MD 20706
www.rowman.com

Falcon and FalconGuides are registered trademarks and Make Adventure Your Story is a trademark of The Rowman & Littlefield Publishing Group, Inc.

Distributed by NATIONAL BOOK NETWORK

Photos by Buck Tilton and Christine Conners unless noted otherwise.
Illustrations by Christine Conners

Maps by The Rowman & Littlefield Publishing Group, Inc.

British Library Cataloguing in Publication Information available

Library of Congress Cataloging-in-Publication Data

Names: Tilton, Buck, author. | Conners, Christine, author.
Title: Outdoor skills for kids / Buck Tilton and Christine Conners.
Description: Essex, Connecticut : Falcon Guides, [2024]
Identifiers: LCCN 2023044120 (print) | LCCN 2023044121 (ebook) | ISBN 9781493073863 (paperback) | ISBN 9781493073870 (epub)
Subjects: LCSH: Wilderness survival—Juvenile literature. | Outdoor recreation for children—Juvenile literature.
Classification: LCC GV200.5 .T53 2024 (print) | LCC GV200.5 (ebook) | DDC 613.6/9—dc23/20231018
LC record available at https://lccn.loc.gov/2023044120
LC ebook record available at https://lccn.loc.gov/2023044121

♾️™ The paper used in this publication meets the minimum requirements of American National Standard for Information Sciences—Permanence of Paper for Printed Library Materials, ANSI/NISO Z39.48-1992.

Important: Never ever put yourself
in a dangerous situation to test
the information in this book.
If you want to practice,
do it in your backyard
with an adult watching.

CONTENTS

INTRODUCTION

Nobody who goes out there thinks they are not coming back. But every year it happens. Some people don't come back. Maybe they get lost, or get too cold, or have an accident, or get sick—or a lot of other unexpected stuff. This book is about coming back. And it's about coming back in as good a shape as possible.

When dangerous events occur in the outdoors, those who survive most often have two things with them. One is a set of skills specific to outdoor survival. This book will help you learn those skills. The other thing is a positive attitude. As your skills increase and improve, so will your attitude. Remember, you are going to be OK.

PLAN TO GO INTO THE OUTDOORS

Do not go alone. Go with at least one parent or guardian, or with an adult you and your parents know and trust—or both. Someone not going with you needs to know exactly where you're going and when you plan to return. Do not change your plans after you get out there.

Make sure this person knows who to contact to initiate a search-and-rescue operation if you don't return. Gather information about the area you intend to visit. Pack gear and clothing in preparation for the worst possible conditions you could expect to encounter.

Safety Tip: Leave an Itinerary

Leave an itinerary! An itinerary is a note that provides important details about your journey. Before leaving on a wilderness adventure, you and your adult hiking buddy should provide a responsible adult (a person not going on the trip) essential information about your plans. This isn't a rule just for kids—adults should always do this too!

An itinerary should include:

- Date and time you plan to leave and return.
- Where your group will be hiking and the trail(s) you plan to use.
- Where you plan to camp if you are staying overnight.
- Names and contact information for everyone on the trip.

RAFAEL BEN-ARI

Always tell an adult where you are going!

PACK THE 11 ESSENTIALS

With these 11 important items, you can safely spend a night out in the outdoors even if you didn't intend to when you left home. These essentials need to be in your backpack, not a backpack someone else is carrying. In other words, these things need to be with *you*.

1. Extra clothing (bright colors)
2. Extra food
3. Water and a means to disinfect it
4. Emergency shelter (such as a space blanket)
5. Map and compass
6. First aid kit
7. Flashlight and extra batteries
8. Fire-starting materials (waterproof matches, a lighter)
9. Sun protection (such as sunglasses, sunscreen, and a hat)
10. Knife (if your parents approve)
11. Whistle

THE 11 ESSENTIALS GAME

Can you identify which of these items are not considered one of the 11 essentials?

1

BREAKERMAXIMUS

2

CAVAN IMAGES/RACHEL BELL

3

HAGEPHOTO

4

WARRENGOLDSWAIN

5

ROBERTPRZYBYSZ

6

RUKAWAJUNG

7

EMS-FORSTER-PRODUCTIONS

8

ZHANNA DANILOVA

9

OSAKAWAYNE STUDIOS

10

VUK SARIC

11

ELVIRA KASHAPOVA

12

RBKOMAR

ANSWER CHECK:

1   Extra clothing is essential.
2   Extra food is essential.
3   Water and a means to disinfect it is essential.
4   Emergency shelter (such as a space blanket) is essential.
5   First aid kit is essential.
6   Flashlight and extra batteries are essential.
7   Incorrect item is the cell phone. A cell phone could be helpful in a survival situation, but it is not considered essential because it is unreliable. Cell phones can break, run out of batteries, or have little to no coverage in the backcountry.
8   Sun protection (such as sunglasses and sunscreen) is essential.
9   A knife (if your parents approve) is essential.
10 Map and compass are essential.
11 Whistle is essential.
12 Fire-starting materials (such as matches and lighter) are essential.

Part One
Getting Lost—
and Found

WHAT IF YOU . . .

START TO FEEL PANIC

Do something. There are plenty of ideas about what you can do in this book. If you're not alone, talk to the people with you. Tell stories. Sing songs. Don't worry about what will happen when you're found. You might feel afraid that you'll be in trouble. It will not happen. When you are found, everyone is going to be very happy. You will not be punished for getting lost.

OKSANA SHUFRYCH

SURVIVAL TIP: COPING WITH FEAR

Did you know that your brain is your most important survival tool? Having a positive mental attitude can improve your chances of survival!

Three characteristics survivors have in common:

They don't give up.

They do whatever it takes to survive.

They maintain a positive attitude in a challenging situation.

Being scared in a survival situation is natural. When you're in danger, your body automatically turns on its fight-or-flight response. This system sets off many physical changes that prepare you to either defend yourself (fight) or escape the situation (flight).

Let's say the legendary Bigfoot walked into your classroom one day. How would you feel? A little scared maybe?! In addition to that emotion of fear, your fight-or-flight system would cause your heart to beat faster, your thoughts to race, your palms to become sweaty, and your muscles to tense up. Those noticeable physical changes (and many others you can't feel) would help you if you need to run from Bigfoot (flight) or defend yourself (fight).

Did you know that your mind can create that same fight-or-flight response without ever encountering Bigfoot? Just believing Bigfoot might walk into your classroom can also trigger the fight-or-flight response! So, the same fight-or-flight response that can help save your life in a real survival situation can also kick in when you are safe, and make you afraid when you don't need to be.

You can stop your body's fear response by sending it calming messages like:

> I am safe.
>
> This will pass.
>
> I am strong.
>
> I can handle this.
>
> I'm a survivor.

Other things you can do to knock out fear are:

> Focus on survival—build a shelter, find water, signal for help, etc.
>
> Take slow deep breaths.
>
> Whistle or sing songs.
>
> Pray.
>
> Make up jokes or stories.
>
> Imagine you are in your favorite place.
>
> Invent a new outdoor game.

Remember: You are strong!

Being afraid is natural in a survival situation, but when there is no immediate danger, calm your mind so you can focus on what needs to be done to survive.

GET LOST IN THE WOODS

Because you were paying attention when you read the first part of this book, you know that someone knows you're out there. You also know that as soon as they realize you are not where you are supposed to be, people are going to be out searching for you. Your job is to make it as easy for the searchers as possible. You make it easier if you stay in one spot. It's much more difficult for searchers to find a moving target. And it's much safer for you to stay in one place than to wander without knowing where you're going.

If you are not alone, everyone needs to stay together. Everyone needs to stay as visible as possible. Put on any bright-colored clothing that you're not wearing. Keep all the stuff you have that is bright colored out in the open or hanging from the limb of a tree or the top of a bush.

Relax. Sit down. Get as comfortable as possible. Collect your thoughts. Listen for the sounds of searchers. Remember you're going to be OK.

There is a chance you might have to wait a long time. Yes, there is even a chance you might have to stay out overnight. You are going to learn a lot about how to do that soon.

TETRA IMAGES—ERIK ISAKSON

SURVIVAL TIP: HUG A TREE

Hug a Tree is a program designed to remind you to stop where you are in the event you get lost. It's not really about "hugging" trees, but about staying put if you get lost. (Bonus survival tip: If you're in cactus country, don't hug a cactus because that's not going to go well for you.) Hug a Tree means you find a safe place and just wait for people to find you. Hugging is optional.

It's really important not to travel when you get lost, because it makes it harder for people to find you. The reason is searchers don't know what direction you may have traveled from the point you were last seen. You could have traveled in any direction from your starting point, so that means they have to search a whole area of a circle to find you when you move.

The chart on the next page calculates how much the search area expands if you keep walking after you realize you are lost. For example, if you walk only 1 mile away from where you got lost, searchers will have to cover an extra 3.14 square miles to try to find you. But if you walk 10 miles away from where you got lost, searchers would have to cover more than 314 square miles of land to try to find you! You can see why it's super important for you to find a safe place and wait for help.

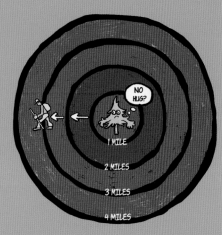

If you continue walking after you get lost, the area people must search to find you dramatically expands the size of the circle, making it more difficult to find you.

Miles Traveled	Approximate Search Area in Square Miles
1 mile	3 square miles
2 miles	13 square miles
3 miles	28 square miles
4 miles	50 square miles
5 miles	79 square miles
6 miles	113 square miles
7 miles	154 square miles
8 miles	201 square miles
9 miles	254 square miles
10 miles	314 square miles

GET LOST IN THE MOUNTAINS

Do all the things you read about if you Get Lost in the Woods. Keep in mind that walking in the rough terrain of mountains is usually riskier than walking in the woods. There are more chances to fall over something or down a slope. So it's especially important to stay in one place.

The ground in the mountains is almost always colder than when you're lower in elevation. Insulate yourself from the ground as much as possible. Sit on your pack and your spare socks and your food bag (after you take the food out—well, you understand).

If the wind blows, get out of it as much as you can. Shelter behind a rock or in a low spot on the ground or behind a stand of scrubby mountain bushes. Make yourself as small as you can so the wind whips away less of your body heat.

KONG DING CHEK

SURVIVAL TIP: DON'T HIDE FROM RESCUERS

Sometimes when kids get lost, they hide from the very people trying to find them. Hiding can make it difficult to be found.

WALDRU

If you go missing, your family and lots of nice strangers will be trying to find you. These strangers might include park rangers, search and rescue employees, volunteers, police officers, and even dogs! You've probably been taught "stranger danger" and that you should avoid people who are strangers to you. That's a good rule, but when you get lost, a lot of strangers, the good ones, are going to be looking for you.

Rescuers might be making lots of loud noises. They might arrive on motorcycles, on horseback, or in helicopters. They may try to talk to you using a loudspeaker. These noises might scare you, but be brave and don't hide!

If you hear people calling your name, respond with your voice or with your whistle. Blow your whistle hard three times. Rest. Blow it again three times. Repeat as necessary until they find you.

You might be afraid of getting in trouble because you broke a rule or didn't listen to an adult. Nobody will be mad at you. In fact, they are going to be very happy when they find you! They will probably even take you out for your favorite treat when it's over!

Make sure they can find you!

PRAETORIANPHOTO

GET LOST IN THE DESERT

Yep, do all those things you read about if you Get Lost in the Woods. There are more things to do in the desert.

Conserve your sweat, not your water. When you're thirsty, drink. Your body will store what it doesn't immediately need. Find or create shade and stay in it when the sun is out. Limit all physical activity. Remember, you want to sweat as little as possible.

Do not eat anything unless it has a lot of water in it, such as juicy fruit. Digesting other foods increases your need for water. Do not talk any more than you have to. Breathe through your nose, not your mouth. Talking and breathing through your mouth cause you to lose some water. Do not undress. Loose, baggy clothing reduces sweat loss. As you know now, make your site as visible as possible and stay put.

Fun Fact: NASAR

The National Association for Search and Rescue (NASAR) trains, organizes, certifies, and coordinates people who want to be involved in search and rescue all across America. You could become an expert rescuer! Find out more at https://nasar.org.

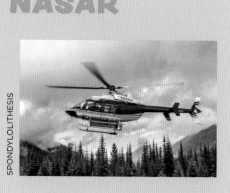

SPONDYLOLITHESIS

MUST SLEEP ON THE GROUND

Look for the driest ground. Assuming you don't have a sleeping pad, you need to construct a "bed" that will keep you dry. It's the moisture that can hurt you. Pile up dry material: leaves, pine needles, moss, duff from the forest floor. You can break off small, green boughs and lay them with the curved side up. If possible, pile your material 3 or 4 feet deep. You can burrow into the pile and end up with a bed and a blanket. If there is only soggy ground where you are, look for logs in order to build a "raft" to sleep on. Where two trees have fallen close together, you might be able to construct a raised platform over soggy ground by bridging the gap between the two trees with branches.

Survived!

In 1990 a 9-year-old boy named Michael became separated from his brothers on a hike at Mount Laguna, California. Michael had taken a Hug a Tree class and knew to stay put. That night, the temperature dropped to 36° F, which is only 4 degrees above freezing. To stay warm, Michael burrowed himself into a soft pile of pine needles. He was found alive and well, 16 hours later.

EVGENIY PRIYMACK

Wear a hat and snuggle if you're cold.

FEEL COLD WHEN YOU'RE TRYING TO SLEEP

If you are insulated from the ground (see Must Sleep on the Ground), be sure you're wearing all the clothes you have with you. Wearing a hat will make you feel warmer. Wear extra socks on your hands. Stick your feet into your pack. Even sleeping with your sunglasses on can keep a tiny bit more heat in. Snuggle up against any other people who are with you. Sleep beside trees, bushes, or rocks to block any wind. If you still feel a chill, get up and do a few jumping jacks to generate heat. It probably won't be your best night ever, but you will be OK.

SURVIVAL TIP: HIKING BUDDIES!

You should always include a responsible adult in all your adventures because it's never safe for children to travel alone! But hiking buddies aren't just for kids. It's recommended that adults have another adult with them on their adventures too.

Hiking buddies provide an extra layer of safety in the outdoors. Imagine if you tripped over a log and sprained your ankle? Your hiking buddy would be there to help you back to safety.

THOMAS BARWICK

Always bring an adult with you on your adventures.

NEED EMERGENCY SHELTER IN THE WOODS

Think small. A small shelter is more easily heated by your body and easier to build. Conservation of body heat is critical to survival. One thing that means is you must stay as dry as possible. A tarp, space blanket, even a large garbage bag supported by sticks or poles will provide a roof. Look also for shelter under dense, overhanging branches or under a fallen tree. If you build a roof out of bushes, tree limbs, or tall grasses, work from the bottom up and make certain that the higher layers drain precipitation onto the lower layers and not inside the shelter.

Face the shelter away from the wind and close off the opposite end. When possible, face the open end toward a reflecting surface, such as a large rock or rocky cliff. A fire between shelter and reflector will heat the shelter. If the ground is not dry, cover it with dry material. If there is nothing else available for a shelter, bury yourself in leaves, pine needles, or other forest debris. With a group, huddle, like spoons in a drawer.

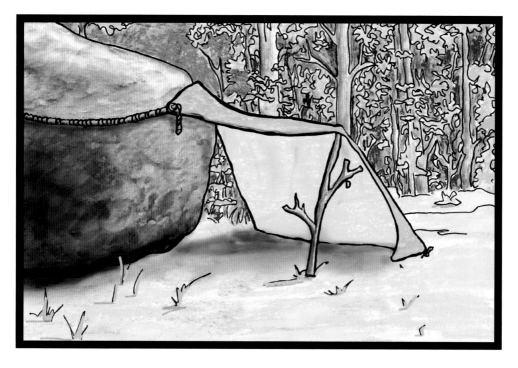

Survived!

In 2023 a plane crashed, leaving four siblings to survive for 40 days in the dense Colombian Amazon rainforest. The survivors, Lesley (13), Soleiny (9), Tien (5), and Cristin (1), are members of a group of indigenous people who from a very young age learn how to survive in the forest. It is these skills that saved their lives!

The children ate fruits and nuts they found in the jungle and flour that was found on the plane. (The flour was extra food, one of the 11 essentials!) Lesley, the oldest, added water to the flour to make a drink for baby Cristin. She was clever and used a leaf to drip the mixture into the baby's mouth. To make a shelter, the children piled banana leaves on top of mosquito netting and a tarp to stay protected and warm against the constant rain.

One hundred and fifty soldiers and their dogs teamed up with local volunteers to find them. Food boxes were dropped from helicopters, one of which the children happily found. Searchers also blasted a recorded message from their grandmother telling the kids to remain calm and stay put. (Remember Hug a Tree?)

Their previous knowledge of the jungle and the heroism of Lesley, the oldest sister, is credited with saving their lives!

Tree pit shelter

NEED EMERGENCY SHELTER IN THE SNOW

In a snowy forest, try to make a tree pit shelter. Look for a tree with overhanging branches that have caught and kept snow from collecting deeply around the trunk. Remove any snow that has collected around the trunk. Use the snow you dig out as additional roofing and walls for your shelter.

If there are no trees, dig a simple trench.

Dig with ski tails, snowshoes, pots or pans, even your gloved hands. Try for a depth of about 3 feet. If the snowpack is thin, look for snow drifted or blown to a deeper depth. Make the trench just a bit longer than you are tall and only a little wider than your shoulders. Cover the trench's bottom with whatever you can use for insulation: your pack, extra clothes, green pine boughs, and so on. Skis, ski poles, or snowshoes placed across the trench will help support a space blanket, tarp, even a large garbage bag as a roof. Anchor the edges of the roof with snow. Leave a small entryway open at one end.

SURVIVAL TIP: TRAIL SIGNS

On well-traveled trails, you will notice different types of signs that can help you stay on course. These were put there by previous hikers or park employees to make it easier for you to follow the trail. Keep an eye out for post signs, blazes, cairns, flags, or even pieces of ribbon. Here are some examples of what you might see.

Post signs

When available, post signs are usually the best way to navigate a trail. Post signs are common in places where a lot of people like to hike, or where trees are scarce. If you're lucky, your trail will be full of these useful guides. They can provide important information about the trail you're on, the distance to the next milestone, and how to get back to the parking lot. If you have a trail map with you, you can use these signs to help determine your location.

PAMELA JOE MCFARLANE

JACOB KUPFERMAN

SIMON MCGILL

Blazes and Markers

The next best method for navigating trails are blazes. Blazes are marks found on trees or prominent objects on the trail. (See pages 32 and 33 on reading blazes to learn what these symbols mean.)

WIKTORD

PAULA SIERRA

MARC GUITARD

Cairns are piles of rocks that have been left by other hikers to help guide you on the path. These are particularly useful when no trees are available. Sometimes people just like to build cairns for fun, so make sure they are in fact part of your trail.

Sometimes you might see plastic ribbons on trees. You have to be a tad careful when navigating with ribbons because they can have more than one meaning. Parks and forest service employees will sometimes mark trees for cutting using ribbons, which can make navigating with ribbons confusing. But ribbons are used as trail guides too. Use your best judgment when navigating with ribbons and use them only when other types of signs aren't available.

Survived!

In 1984 in Shenandoah National Park in Virginia, Shawn, a 10-year-old boy, got lost when he separated from his hiking party. He had learned to hug a tree from a program in his school and decided to stop walking so he "wouldn't get more lost." His hiking party found him only a short time after he was lost.

RUN OUT OF WATER

Go 3 days without water and you're in serious trouble. This doesn't happen often. But if it does, the advice in this section requires you to break an important rule. The rule says "Stay Put, and Wait for Help to Come." You are going to move.

Collect rainwater.

Move carefully downhill, the way water runs. Follow animal tracks or watch the evening flights of birds; both often lead to water. Stop periodically and listen: You may hear water running. You might find water by digging a hole at the outside of bends in dry streambeds. If it has rained recently, you might also find water in hollows in rocks or other places where rainwater collects. If it rains, catch as much water as possible in whatever is available: pots, cups, tarps, even clothing (you can wring out the water). Just before sunrise, gather the dew that collects on leaves, flowers, metal surfaces, or anything else.

With a sheet of plastic, you can build a solar still: Dig a hole 3 feet wide and 1½ feet deep, place a container in the middle, cover the hole with plastic secured on its edges, and weight the center of the plastic to form an inverted cone. Water will condense on the inside of the plastic and drip into the container. Placing green plants under the plastic will increase the amount of water you get.

Solar still

NEED TO DISINFECT WATER

Boil it. Water heated to the boiling point is free of disease-causing germs. A lengthy boil is not required.

Or *filter it*. Different water filters accomplish different things. Some filters strain out only protozoa, such as Giardia and Cryptosporidium (both of which can make you very sick); others strain out protozoa and bacteria. No filter strains out viruses, however, although some are coated with an iodine resin that may kill viruses. Before you buy a water filter, read the directions carefully to learn exactly what it can and can't do.

Or *use chemical disinfectants*. Some chemicals, called halogens, are very good at killing almost everything harmful in water. Iodine and chlorine are the safest and most effective chemicals (iodine in partic-ular is often the preferred chemical because it stores better and reacts less with organic compounds in water), but no chemical guarantees water safe from Cryptosporidium. Follow the directions on the label of any chemical you use.

Boil snow or water.

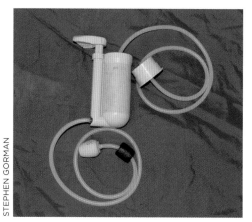

Water filter

Chemical disinfectants

A tributary stream is a smaller stream that flows into a bigger one.

FIND WATER BUT CAN'T DISINFECT IT

Drink from small tributary streams, the water that flows into a big stream or river, instead of the main flow. If you're way out there, far from most people, water in small streams has a better chance of being safe than water from other sources. If possible, follow tributaries uphill to their source, if you can follow it safely. A spring will be your best bet.

Drink from the surface of a deep, still pool. If you find one, drink from the middle, as far from the banks as safely possible. But be very careful not to fall in. Water tumbling over rocks looks appealing, but the tumbling action stirs up germs in the water. Drink from pools surrounded by healthy, green plants, not from pools surrounded by barren ground or, even worse, the bleached bones of animals. Dig a hole at the outside of bends of streams. Water that seeps into the hole will be at least partially filtered.

Survived!

In 2004 three children in the North Coast of Australia survived for 6 days alone after their family's boat capsized in rough seas.

The siblings, Norita (10), Stephen (12), and Ellis (15), initially swam 5.6 miles (wow!) through shark- and crocodile-infested waters to a rock outcrop where they waited without food or water for 3 days. Due to the lack of resources on the rock, the children made the critical decision to swim another mile to a deserted island where they waited (remember Hug a Tree?). Once on the island they were able to live on native plums, oysters, shellfish, and coconuts until they were rescued by their uncle.

The children's aunt credits their survival with the fact that children growing up on the Torres Strait are taught basic survival skills at a young age. These people wisely believe that "all the kids must know how to survive in times of being lost."

SURVIVAL TIP: TOPO MAPS

Safe trips begin by studying the map of the area before you leave.

Topographical ("topo") maps are specifically designed to help you in the backcountry. Topo maps use contour lines to show the rise and fall of the earth's surface and include important features to help you recognize where you are, like trails, peaks, rivers, roads, lakes, and vegetation. These important features make the topo map and compass one of your 11 essentials!

It takes practice to read a topo map, but here's some things to get you started:

Contour lines: Contour lines give you important information about the elevation of the land around you. The contour lines of a mountain might look something like this:

What the actual mountain would look like in person is more like this:

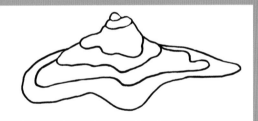

Land features to look for:

Roads—usually shown as double black lines

Green areas—areas where there are trees and plants

Ridge (elevated crest)—contours come together then separate

Summit/high point—contour lines loop around the peak

Trails—dashed black lines

Steep area —contour lines are close together

Valleys—contours bend into the hill

Streams—blue lines

Lakes/ponds—blue areas indicate bodies of water

Flat areas—contoured areas are spaced out

CAN YOU READ THIS MAP?

Learning to read topo maps will take time and practice, but you probably already know more than you realize! Use the list on the previous page to see if you can match the numbers with the correct land feature. Check your answers below.

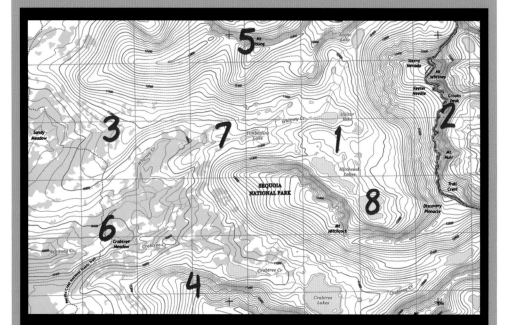

Number	Land Feature
1	trail
2	lake
3	stream
4	summit
5	flat area
6	steep area
7	ridge
8	valley

NEED TO BUILD A FIRE

Gather a large pile of dry material—dead grass, old pine needles, paper-like bark—to use as tinder. Tinder is small stuff that burns easily. Next, gather a lot of kindling: small, dry twigs. Kindling is bigger than tinder but still burns pretty quickly. Then gather several armloads of fuel: dry pieces of wood, wood that snaps when you break it. Gather more material than you think you'll need. Build your fire on dry, non-vegetated soil. If the wind is blowing, make a windbreak of rocks or logs. When wind and fire combine, it can be very dangerous. Build a pyramid of tinder, fluffing it so air can circulate through. Over the tinder build a loose pyramid of kindling. When all is ready, set a flame to the tinder. When the kindling is fully involved, start adding progressively larger pieces of fuel, arranging things loosely to allow air to flow through. Add fuel slowly until the fire is the desired size, but keep it small. A small fire saves fuel and keeps you just as warm as a large one if you sit close. And please remember that putting out fires you build is very important. When you walk away for the last time from a fire, be sure it is completely out.

Build your fire away from vegetation or flammable objects. A ring of rocks helps keep the fire from spreading.

SURVIVAL TIP: COMPASS

The earth has an invisible magnetic field called the geomagnetic field. The main arrow on your compass (usually in red) is called the magnetic needle and always points toward magnetic north. (Metal objects like knives and belt buckles can affect the accuracy of your magnetic needle, so make sure they are out of the way when you use your compass.)

You've probably already learned that there are four cardinal directions: north, east, south, and west. In case you have trouble remembering the order, you can use this memory trick: "Never Eat Soggy Waffles." Not only is that excellent advice, but it also helps you remember that "north, east, south, and west" are the cardinal directions found *clockwise on your compass.*

True north is always shown as the top location on all official maps. Magnetic north is not true north, and the difference between magnetic north and true north is called the "declination." The declination number can be found in the legend on a topo map or online. When working with a map, ask an adult to help you adjust your compass to the declination specific to your location.

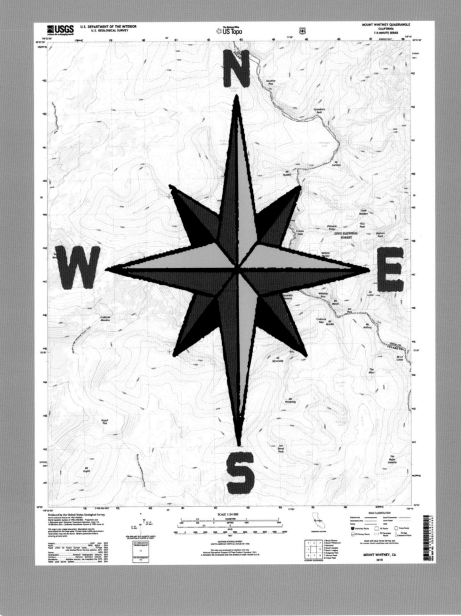

The Parts of a Compass
Here are the key things to look for on a compass:

Direction-of-travel arrow: This is the direction you want to go. You will align the direction you want to go using the directionals on your bezel ring.

Magnifying lens: The magnifying lens allows you to see fine details on your map.

Rotating bezel: The bezel is a ring that rotates and shows NESW as well as 360 degrees.

Magnetic needle: The magnetic needle always points to magnetic north.

Orienting arrow: The orienting arrow is used to orient the bezel. It is an outline shaped to fit around the magnetic needle that helps to anchor north.

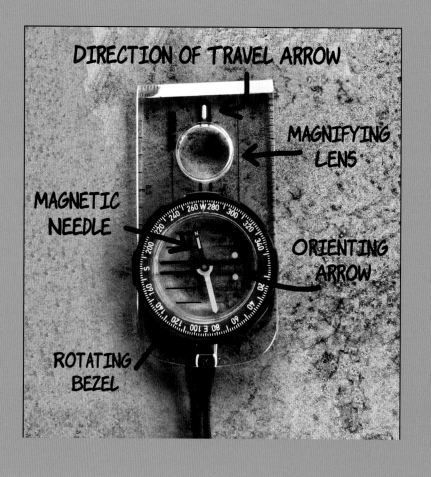

DIRECTION OF TRAVEL ARROW

MAGNIFYING LENS

MAGNETIC NEEDLE

ORIENTING ARROW

ROTATING BEZEL

USING YOUR COMPASS

Find magnetic north: Let's start by finding magnetic north! Hold your compass flat in the palm of your hand directly in front of you with the direction-of-travel arrow facing away from you.

Turning the bezel ring, move the "N" (north) to align with the direction-of-travel arrow. Now turn your whole body around until the magnetic needle sits perfectly over the orienting arrow. You have now found magnetic north!

ERIK ISAKSON

Magnetic north

Find magnetic east: Now let's find east! Turn the bezel ring to line up the "E" (east) with the direction-of-travel arrow. Once set, hold the compass flat in the palm of your hand in front of your body with the direction-of-travel arrow facing away from you. Now turn your whole body around until the magnetic needle is over the orienting arrow. You are now facing east! Repeat these same steps to find south and west.

Carry your compass with you throughout the day and practice finding the different directionals around you!

LINED UP TO POINT EAST

Magnetic east

RUN OUT OF FOOD

It's not fun to be hungry, but it takes a long time to die of starvation. Stay warm and find water, and you'll survive for weeks without food. It's always safest to only eat food you *know is OK for humans.*

If you need food, look for plants, but remember that plants other animals eat may not be safe for you to eat. Bugs, birds, and other beasts can often eat food humans can't. Never eat any mushrooms you find. If you're unsure, follow these five steps—and follow them in this order:

1. Inspect potential food and test only healthy-looking plants: no slime, no bug-eaten edges.
2. Crush a portion and smell it. Discard plants that smell bitter, like vinegar, or otherwise bad.
3. Rub juice from the crushed plant on the inside of your elbow. If it irritates your skin, discard the plant.
4. Chew a small portion of the plant, then spit it out. Do not swallow it. Wait a few minutes. If there is any discomfort—irritation, burning, stinging—discard the plant.
5. Chew and swallow a small portion, then wait about 5 hours without eating anything else. If there is no stomach discomfort after 5 hours, the plant is almost always safe to eat.

To vary your diet, eat insects. Yuck, yep, but they are nutritious and safe to eat when roasted on hot rocks or boiled.

KRISTINAVF

NEED TO SIGNAL FOR HELP

Make yourself as visible as possible. Contrast is the key element in signaling. Bright orange against the dark of a forest, for instance, creates a contrast. Look for an open area—a meadow, an open ridgeline—where you'll be seen from all directions. Smoky fires by day and bright fires by night are effective signals. After the fire is blazing, add damp wood to make the most smoke. The letter X on the ground is rarely seen in nature and is always a good signal. Make the X from large pieces of wood, brightly colored material (clothes, camping equipment), or rocks. You could also stamp out the letter in snow. Make your X as large as pos-

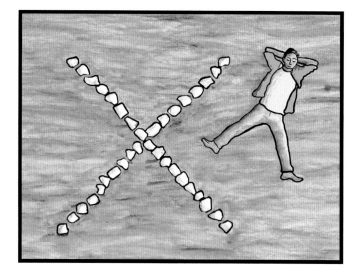

sible. If a plane passes overhead, do not wave your arms. Waving is what friendly people do, not lost people. Stand with arms high and wide, a plea for help. Signal with reflected light: Use a signal mirror or a piece of glass or polished metal.

Fun Fact!

The first compass was invented by the Chinese at some point between the second century BCE and the first century CE. It was first used, not as a navigation tool, but for feng shui, which is the practice of arranging living spaces to create balance with the natural world.

The original compass consisted of a spoon made of magnetized lodestone, which acted like a needle on a compass. The bowl of the spoon was placed in the center of a bronze plate and would align itself with the earth's magnetic field, causing the handle to point south.

RICHCANO

NEED TO USE A SIGNAL MIRROR

Face the target, which might be a passing airplane, a distant car, or anywhere you think help might be.

Hold the mirror in one hand, near your face. Hold your other hand toward the target, arm outstretched. Focus the reflection of the sun on your outstretched hand. Your outstretched hand is now a line of sight. Adjust your outstretched hand and the mirror to direct the reflection toward the target. Remember that even on cloudy days reflected light may be seen for many miles.

CAN YOU READ THE SIGNS?

Blazes are a type of trail marker that help guide you along the path. These can be especially important if your trail is overgrown or under snow. These markings were once carved out of the bark, but today, to protect the trees, they are usually painted. Learning what these signs mean can give you important information about where your trail is headed.

Remember, you should never hike without an adult! If you're lost, stay put and wait for help.

This is the symbol you find at the start of your trail.

This symbol means your trail is moving straight ahead.

This pattern means your trail is turning right.

This pattern means your trail is turning left.

This pattern means another trail is intersecting with your trail. They call the connecting path a spur trail.

The double blaze means you are on two trails that are overlapping one another. The different colors represent the different trails.

This marking means your trail has come to an end. Congratulations, your journey is complete!

NEED TO USE A WHISTLE TO SIGNAL

Sound is an effective signal if there might be someone close enough to hear you. The sound of a whistle will carry farther than your voice, and you can keep blowing long after you have run out of energy to yell. Again, sets of three are a recognized call for help: three evenly spaced blows on a whistle. Count to three to yourself while you are blowing. In between each set of three blows, take a few minutes to listen.

MARTINAN

Survived!

In 2023 a 10-year-old girl named Shunghla survived 24 hours alone in the Cascade Mountains when she got separated while hiking with her family. Her family, volunteers, deputies, dogs, drones, and helicopters all searched for her.

When they didn't find her that day, Shunghla was forced to stay overnight alone in the woods. The temperature that night dropped to 37° F (5 degrees above freezing). Shunghla stayed warm by sleeping between two trees. The sheriff's office praised Shunghla as extraordinarily resourceful and resilient.

Prior to getting lost, Shunghla and her family enjoyed spending time in the forest, where she had learned basic outdoor skills. But her most important survival skill was her ability to stay calm when she got lost. Shunghla didn't panic when she realized she was lost. She told the authorities that she knew what she needed to do and maintained a level head about it.

GET STUCK IN A VEHICLE IN COLD WEATHER

Unless the driver knows exactly where to go for help, it's not far, *and* the weather permits safe travel, stay with the vehicle. Searchers find vehicles much easier than they find hikers. If snow is falling, periodically brush it from the roof and hood to make the vehicle more visible. Run the heater no more than 5 minutes every half hour. Always keep windows on both sides of the vehicle cracked when the engine is running. Never fall asleep while the engine is running, and make sure the tailpipe is clear of snow. Without a sleeping bag, wrap yourself in newspapers, magazines, floor mats, carpeting, or anything else you can find in the vehicle. You can also cut the stuffing from the seats to use as insulation. People have survived more than a week in snowbound vehicles.

ISABEL PAVIA

CRAZY BLAZES TO THE POT OF GOLD GAME

On pieces of scratch paper, draw several sets of the following blaze symbols from Can You Read The Signs:

Start
Straight ahead
Turn right
Turn left
Trail end

On a separate piece of paper, draw a pot of gold. Have your buddy close their eyes while you strategically place the blaze symbols around your campsite in a wacky way that leads to the pot of gold drawing. Hide the pot of gold drawing so it's tricky to find. Double-check that your symbols make sense!

When your buddy opens their eyes, have them use their blaze reading skills to follow your path to the pot of gold.

Take turns moving the pot of gold and changing the paths to find it.

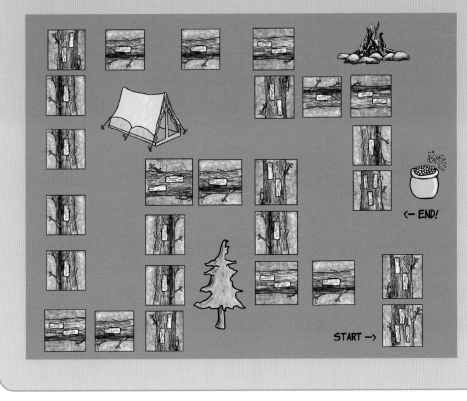

Part Two
Running into Natural Problems

WHAT IF YOU . . .

GET CHILLED IN COLD WEATHER

There are different degrees of "chilled." In all cases, drink some water and eat a snack, empowering your body to warm up. If you are only slightly chilled but are physically fit, well hydrated, and well nourished, you'll probably be OK if you just add a layer of clothing and exercise until the chill goes away. For deeper chills, the kind that cause violent shivering, stop and change into dry clothes, bundling yourself against the cold. Then rest, well insulated from the ground, until the chill goes away.

IMGORTHAND

Fun Fact: Orienteering USA

If you enjoy hiking and navigation, you can join a local orienteering club! Orienteering is the competitive sport of backcountry navigation and is tons of fun! It's like hiking and a treasure hunt combined. Using a map that has designated checkpoints, your goal is to find all the checkpoints as quickly as possible. It's a great way to get some exercise and improve your backcountry navigation skills!

Tip: In some areas of the country, you can find permanent orienteering parks that are available year-round. The maps for these courses are found online.

Go to www.orienteeringusa.org to find orienteering activities in your area.

RAWPIXEL

NEED TO DRY WET CLOTHES

Wet synthetics (such as polyester and nylon), though uncomfortable, will hold in most of your body heat. If you're wearing synthetic material, and if you're fit, hydrated, and well fed, you can keep exercising (for instance, keep hiking) in wet clothes, and they'll dry on your body. Wet wool holds in a lot of body heat, but it seldom dries entirely on your body. Cotton will never dry while you're wearing it—unless it's a hot, dry day.

Hung over a bush or tree limb, wet clothes will eventually dry, even on a freezing cold day. They'll dry faster if the wind is blowing. If you're in a hurry, build a fire, but don't hang clothes directly over the flames. It's too hot, and they'll singe or, worse, burn. Hang them over something like a rack of sticks. If you're patient, hold them near the heat. Never leave clothes unattended near a fire. Check them often. If the clothes feel hot, they're too near the heat. If they feel warm, you're doing it just right.

NEED TO THAW AND DRY FROZEN CLOTHES

If only your outer layer is frozen, you can safely keep wearing the clothes. You're probably still warm and at least relatively dry at skin level. A frozen synthetic outer layer will thaw and dry while you're exercising and generating heat. On a cold, dry day, even frozen outer wool layers may thaw and dry on your body.

But when the moisture reaches down to inner layers, you need to get out of frozen clothes as soon as possible, before your body temperature starts to drop. Hung in the open (over ski tips, over tree limbs), frozen clothes will thaw and dry even when the mercury has plunged to well below zero. The process is called sublimation, the changing of a solid (the ice) to a vapor without a liquid phase in between. Clothes will thaw and dry faster near a fire (see Need to Dry Wet Clothes). If it's possible to build two fires, it might be wisest to take off most or all of your frozen layers and stand in between the fires to keep warm as the clothes are drying. Otherwise, it's best to dry wet clothes piece by piece.

BINABINA

GET NUMB FINGERS OR TOES IN THE COLD

Warm them up immediately. Numb body parts are well on their way to becoming frozen body parts. If your fingers or toes are only slightly numb, warm them by swinging your arms or legs vigorously to restore circulation. If that fails, remove your gloves or boots and socks and place your cold body parts against warm body parts. You can place your fingers in your armpits or groin, or your feet against the abdomen of someone else. Skin-to-skin contact will adequately warm the numb parts. Do not rub numb fingers and toes. Do not hold them near a high heat source, such as a blazing fire. Rubbing and high heat may damage numb body parts.

FINWAL

GET CAUGHT IN A BLIZZARD

If you're prepared with proper clothing or, even better, if you have or can construct shelter, hunker down and wait it out. To keep traveling is to invite injury or get lost. If the snow is deep enough, construct a small snow shelter. Even if it's only a shallow trench, you'll be out of the wind (see Need Emergency Shelter in Snow).

If you noted major landmarks prior to the storm—ridges, cliffs, big trees, ravines—you might choose to head for the landmark if you can see it. But swirling snow makes it difficult to be sure of what you're seeing. Move only if you're sure of the direction and you think you'll have more shelter when you reach your destination. If you do move, don't overexert yourself. You don't want to burn up your life-sustaining energy or get wet with sweat.

SURVIVAL TIP: THE RULE OF THREES

The Rule of Threes is an old and important reminder of your priorities in a survival situation. The threes (minutes, days, weeks) are not exact, but they do help you remember what to think about and in what order.

ALOHA_17

You can live only about 3 minutes without air. Yes, keep breathing!

PETERAPRAHAMIAN

You can live about 3 hours without shelter (in extreme cold). Find ways to stay warm, dry, out of the wind, and as comfortable as possible.

NIGEL_WALLACE

You can live about 3 days without water. Thirst might be a problem, but it will not be serious right away.

JUSTIN SMITH

You can live about 3 weeks without food. Hunger might bother you, but it will not harm you for a fairly long time.

GET CAUGHT IN AN AVALANCHE

Throw off everything you can. Large packs, skis, and ski poles might drag you under. Retaining small day packs, however, may offer flotation, which is good. As you are swept away, swim. Use any motion you can to keep your head above "water." If you feel your feet hit something solid, push off aggressively to regain the surface. If your head goes under, keep your mouth shut and do not breathe. Keep your airway free of snow. As the slide slows down, make energetic efforts to reach the surface. If that isn't working, vigorously try to create a breathing space: Shake your head, try to get a hand up to your face to push the snow away, and wiggle around to make room for your chest to move. Thrust a hand toward the surface. Most victims are found because something shows above the snow.

If you're trapped beneath the snow, survival is more likely if you stay calm. Escape efforts will waste oxygen and energy. Panic increases the need for oxygen.

CHRISTOPHER BELLAMY

Push something through the snow so rescuers can find you.

GET CAUGHT IN A LIGHTNING STORM

Find the safest spot possible. Avoid high places, tall objects, metal objects, open places, open bodies of water, and long electrical conductors such as fences. Seek uniform cover such as a low spot in low, rolling hills or a stand of trees all about the same size—but do not lean against a tree. Assume the lightning safety position: Squat or sit in a tight position on insulating material. Spread groups out, but try to keep everyone in sight. If you can find a deep, dry cave, you may be safer inside than outside, but do not touch the cave walls. If you are near your vehicle, get in and stay in with the windows rolled up.

Lightning safety position

Fun Fact: Cairns

Cairns are those cool man-made stacks of rocks you'll come across in the wilderness. The name "cairn" comes come from the Scottish Gaelic word meaning "heap of stones."

The building of cairns has been around since prehistory and continues to be found all over the world. Cairns can range in size from a simple directional marker to an entire hill of rocks with a chamber!

Globally cairns have been used as altars, as trail markers, to mark burial sites, as landmarks, as coastal navigation aids, and even to bring good luck. Their presence is found woven into different beliefs, customs, rituals, religious ceremonies, classical mythology, and even biblical text.

Unfortunately, many parks forbid guests from making their own cairns for fun. (That's a big bummer, we know!) But there are several good reasons for this. Cairns are often used by the Forest Service as trail guides. If everyone was building cairns, hikers could get lost and confused!

Another reason is that there are often little critters living under the rocks you find on the ground. If you've ever peeked under a rock, you know that rocks provide shelter to reptiles, invertebrates, fish, small mammals, and bugs. Moving these stones can disrupt or hurt the creatures living under them.

Moving rocks can also increase the rate of erosion in the area. Rocks prevent soil, plants, and sand from being washed away.

Survival exception: In a survival situation, rocks can serve as tools for personal defense, signaling for help, and providing shelter against the elements. In a survival situation, don't hesitate to move those rocks!

CONNERS

COME FACE-TO-FACE WITH A WILDFIRE

Wildfires are fast and furious—and terribly destructive. The smell of smoke is often your first warning. Watch over the treetops for trails of smoke rising upward. You need to move quickly away from the fire—but it's not always easy to know which way to go. Wind pushes fire along. If wind is blowing, hurry into the wind. The wind will push the fire away from you. Fires tend to burn uphill. If the ground slopes, hurry downhill.

But if you see fire below you, move uphill. When you reach a high point of the slope, head down the other side of the ridge or hill. When the fire reaches the top, it will slow down. Stay out of gullies because fires tend to speed up in them.

If smoke makes it hard to breathe, and you have water, wet your shirt or a bandanna and hold it over your mouth and nose.

Keep moving until you find help or a place that is safe from the wildfire.

BLOOMBERG CREATIVE

SWISSMEDIAVISION

CAMP IN THE RAIN

When it rains, the main idea, of course, is to stay as dry as possible. Before leaving home, ask about your rain gear and your shelter. Are the seams sealed? Sometimes the seams will be sealed by whoever made the gear. Some gear has to be seam-sealed with a product made for that purpose. Sealed seams are watertight.

Avoid pitching a tent in a depression (a low spot in the ground). It can fill with water. Keep your tent set up with the sides pulled tight. Or, even better, if your tent has a rain fly, keep that tight. A tent set up tight sheds water better. Keep doors and vents at least partially open to allow air to circulate. Circulating air prevents condensation. Heavy condensation will make the inside of your tent wet. Keep your sleeping bag and clothing away from the tent's entrance. Keep your spare clothing and anything else you want to stay dry inside waterproof stuff sacks or plastic bags. Hang a clothesline inside your tent to allow damp clothing to dry while you sleep. In rainy weather, choose a synthetic sleeping bag. It soaks up less water and dries faster than the feathers in a down bag do.

FALL THROUGH THIN ICE

This is important: Don't cross ice that is covering water. If you don't know you are on ice, and you fall through, throw a hand over your nose and mouth to prevent inhaling water. The icy cold will cause a gasping reflex, but if you don't inhale water, you'll be fine—so relax. It's a myth that you'll die from the cold in a few minutes. It takes a half hour for hypothermia to take hold of a dressed person floating in ice water.

But the cold will quickly reduce your coordination, so attempt to get out of the water right away. Spread your arms over the firm edge of the ice hole. Kick aggressively and swim up onto the ice. Once out of the water, do not stand up. Your upright weight might cause the ice to break again. Crawl to safety. Unless you are only minutes from shelter, do not attempt to walk while wet. Get dry now, before the cold sucks away your body heat (see Need to Dry Wet Clothes).

IMGORTHAND

HAVE TO CROSS SWAMPY LAND

You usually find the driest ground near the edges of swamps, especially sloped ground that can drain. If there are stands of trees, they're often growing on slightly elevated, drier ground, which is where you should try to cross. Look for animal trails and follow them when you can. You may be able to step on tussocks (little mounds typically overgrown with grass or brush). But step with care—and do not jump. Tussocks are often unstable and surrounded by small pools of mud and water. It's generally safer to wade through the muck and clean up afterward than to jump from mound to mound. If you walk in the muck, probe ahead with a long stick to avoid holes.

ATOSAN

RBKOMAR

Yell and wave to attract attention!

FALL OUT OF A BOAT

When you feel yourself falling, hold a hand over your nose and mouth so you don't inhale water. Then relax. You'll float to the surface, especially if you're wearing a personal flotation device (PFD)—which is pretty much always a good idea. If no one saw you fall, yell and wave your arms to attract attention. If the boat stops a short distance away, swim to it. And remember, please, if you get tired while you're swimming, stop and roll over onto your back. You can rest and still have plenty of air to breathe. If the boat is returning to you, wait for it. If it's a large boat, wait until a means of climbing aboard is in place or lowered to you, then use it. If it's a small boat, wait until the onboard crew has the craft balanced. Move to the stern (the rear of the boat). Attempting to climb aboard amidships (the middle of the ship) can overturn a small vessel. Hold onto the gunwale (the top edge of the side of a boat) and bob up and down in the water until you have enough momentum to throw your belly up onto the gunwale. Then squirm into the boat. If your attempt to reenter the boat is unsuccessful, hold on while the boat is moved to shallower water.

SURVIVAL TIP: LEARN TO SWIM

The most common reason someone does not survive when they fall into water is because they don't know how to swim. Learning to swim is fun, good exercise, and a really good idea. If you don't know how to swim, please learn. And please, even you can swim, wear a personal flotation device when you're on water.

JASMIN MERDAN

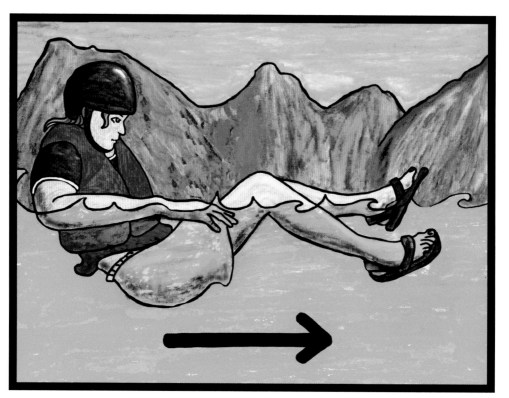

Point your feet downstream to protect your head.

FALL OUT OF A MOVING RAFT

Are you wearing a helmet for safety? If you aren't, you ought to be. When you feel yourself falling, hold a hand over your nose and mouth so you don't inhale water. Falling out of a raft is rarely a serious problem as long as you don't try to stand up and are wearing a personal flotation device. Trying to stand can cause you to snag your feet on the bottom, which is extremely dangerous. After you are floating on the surface, face downstream and bring your feet up to the surface in front of you. This safety position will allow you to push off rocks and other obstacles in the water. In slow-moving water, you might be able to swim back to the raft while maintaining the safety position. Allow someone to pull you back in. In rapids, don't fight the current. Allow the flow to carry you through. As soon as possible, move toward an eddy (a pool of still water) or the nearest bank. People on the raft will come back for you.

ARE IN A BOAT THAT CAPSIZES

Do not leave the boat, unless it sinks. Small boats often float when overturned. If you surface under the boat, stay calm. There is almost always a pocket of air beneath a flipped boat. Relax and get your bearings, then move out from under the boat. In moving water do not attempt to stand up. Move to the upriver end of the boat and hold on until calmer water is reached. In deep, calm water you might be able to right a small craft (such as a canoe), enter it, and "swim" it to shore. In all cases your chances of survival decrease when you leave the boat.

JOHNER IMAGES—WALSTROM, SUSANNE

Stay near your capsized boat.

ARE IN A BOAT THAT GROUNDS

Maintain your balance. Then throw your weight backward with a slight rocking motion to try to slide the boat off the sandbar, rock, or log you're grounded on. In shallow water, try to push off the bottom with a paddle or oar. If you're not alone, have the others shift their weight toward the stern (the rear end of the boat), lifting the bow (the front end of the boat). If all else fails, you'll have to leave the boat (wearing your PFD, of course) in order to lift it off the ground. But remember leaving the boat in fast-moving water is dangerous.

IPPEI NAOI

Rock the boat slowly.

SURVIVAL TIP: RIP CURRENTS

Rip currents happen when waves hit the beach in a specific way that causes the current to move away from the beach. According to the National Oceanic and Atmospheric Administration (NOAA), about 30,000 swimmers are rescued from rip currents each year and 100 people drown. If you ever see a rip current warning sign on the beach, you should not swim there.

Rip currents can be difficult to impossible to see from the beach. But sometimes you can spot a rip current from a high position on the beach. You might notice them as an area where the waves aren't breaking or where the water appears discolored or different.

Rip currents don't pull swimmers underwater, but they do pull swimmers away from the beach. It can be frightening! Even the strongest swimmers can be pulled away by a rip tide.

LISALNGLASSES

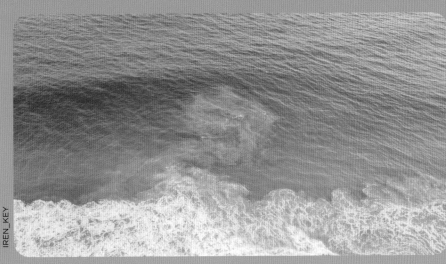

IREN_KEY

Can you spot the rip current in this photo?

If you get pulled into a rip current:

- Don't panic. Panicking has caused people to drown.
- Shout to people on the beach for help.
- Don't fight against the current. Instead, attempt to escape the current by swimming parallel to the shoreline.
- Once you are out of the current, move back toward the beach staying far away from the rip current.
- If at any time you get tired, float on your back and rest.

Part Three
Running into Wild Creatures

WHAT IF YOU . . .

HIKE IN BEAR COUNTRY

Hike and camp in a manner designed to avoid bears. Stay out of areas with signs of bear use, such as bear scat and bear tracks. Avoid areas that smell of decaying meat. Camp in the open. Cook food at least 100 yards from your tent. Camp cleanly: Don't wipe food-stained hands and utensils on clothing, avoid spilling food on the ground, and don't burn leftover food. Pack all food and other strong-smelling items in a separate bag so the smells don't get into the outer pack and clothing. Don't pack fish or greasy food. At night, hang the food and aromatic items out of a bear's reach. Make sure a bear couldn't reach them from the ground or from a tree: Hang them at least 10 feet high and at least 4 feet from the trunk of a tree. Double-check your local wildlife resources for regulations regarding food storage. When hiking, travel in groups of four or more, a group size that discourages bears from approaching. Try never to surprise a bear. Almost all bears will run away if they smell or hear humans before they see them. Traveling with the wind (the wind blows against your back) and making noise will help make bears aware of your proximity.

Prevention is critical to avoid contact with a bear.

DOUGLAS SACHA

Food is suspended overhead to prevent bears and other animals from reaching it.

SURVIVAL TIP: RECOGNIZING SIGNS OF ANIMAL ACTIVITY

Tracking is the ancient art of learning to read the footprints of animals and humans. It was an essential survival skill for ancient peoples and continues to be so today.

If you were to become a professional tracker, you could look at a print and not only determine which animal it's from, but also its sex, its size, its speed of travel, and the direction it was traveling!

Animal tracks are not the only sign that an animal has been in your area. Look for scratch and bite marks on plants or trees.

JILLIAN SUZANNE

Bear claw marks on the bark of trees.

ANDREW PEACOCK

Can you tell what this bear ate today?

Be on the lookout for clumps of feathers, hair, and scat (animal poop).

Animals will create their own paths in the wilderness. These are usually paths that lead to water or food sources and are usually narrower and a little more overgrown. They can sometimes confuse hikers and cause them to leave the main trail.

TODD RYBURN PHOTOGRAPHY

Animals will naturally make their own trails.

AKCHAMCZUK

Can you tell a beaver was here?

Some people wear "bear bells" to warn bears and other animals they are in the area.

ENCOUNTER A BEAR

Back away slowly. Do not run. Do not climb a tree. A bear often turns and runs away. If it doesn't, speak in a calm, quiet voice. Tell the bear to go away. Avoid direct eye contact. Bear behavior is unpredictable, but bears that feel threatened often turn sideways, displaying their size. They may woof aggressively. They may charge toward a threat, then suddenly stop. If a bear does any of this, raise your arms to look bigger and speak louder. If you are in a group, stand close together to maximize your size. Pepper spray might deter a bear that's within 7 to 10 yards.

If a black bear attacks, fight it off, striking at the bear's nose and eyes with rocks, sticks, or your fists. Black bears often retreat from a counterattack. If a grizzly attacks, play dead. Lie on your stomach, clasp your hands protectively behind your neck, press your arms against the sides of your head. If the bear rolls you over, keep rolling until you're belly down again, but stay "dead." Keep playing dead until the bear is long gone.

CONNERS

ENCOUNTER A MOUNTAIN LION

Do not run away. Do not turn your back. Stand up tall and face the animal. Mountain lions prefer a surprise attack, so let it know that you've seen it. In a group, gather everyone close together. Make yourself look as big as possible, holding your arms up, and holding up a jacket or pack.

If the mountain lion crouches and moves closer, show your teeth, yell, and pick up rocks and throw them at the animal. Pick up a stick. A mountain lion crouching low, twitching its tail, and staring intently at you is preparing to attack. If its back leg starts to pump up and down, an attack is certain. If an attack seems imminent, move toward the animal, yelling and striking at its face, but don't step within reach of the lion's claws. If attacked, fight aggressively, striking at the lion's nose, eyes, and ears.

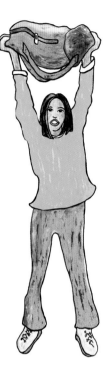

If you see a mountain lion, make your-self look as big as possible.

ENCOUNTER A MOOSE

Back away quickly. A moose that is licking its lips or has its ears laid back and its rump hairs raised is usually on the verge of a charge. Moose may attack aggressively, especially in spring (when baby moose are born), or in the fall. If a moose charges, run away. Try to get behind a large, solid object—a tree or rock—for protection. Keep the object between the moose and you. If its victim falls to the ground, a moose may kick viciously with its forefeet, its favored form of attack, until the victim appears to be no further threat. If you are knocked to the ground, roll into a tight ball, protect your head with your arms, and wait without moving until the moose moves well away.

SCOTT SURIANO

FOOTPRINT TRACKING GUIDE

STAN TEKIELA AUTHOR/NATURALIST/ WILDLIFE PHOTOGRAPHER

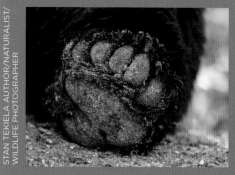

Below is a footprint guide that contains 12 different examples of footprints you might find on your adventures.

The size of the footprint is important for tracking identification. A domestic cat footprint is between 1 and 1½ inches long compared to a cougar footprint, which can look similar but can be as large as 4 inches!

Also note that the front feet of some animals may look very different from their hind (back) feet. They may even look like they came from different animals!

BEAR
HIND 7" FRONT 4.5 "

RACOON
HIND 4" FRONT 2.5"

SNAKE
CLASSIC PATTERN

TURKEY
4"

DEER
2.5" – 3"

HUMAN

RABBIT
FRONT 1" HIND 3.5"

SQUIRREL
HIND 2.25" FRONT 1.5"

BEAVER
HIND 6" FRONT 3"

DUCK ~ 3 "

COUGAR/MOUNTAIN LION
3" TO 3.5"

WOLF 4" – 5"

TRACKING GAME

Real-life footprints are rarely in perfect condition and can be difficult to read in the wild. Using the Footprint Tracking Guide, see how many tracks you can correctly identify! The answers are upside down below.

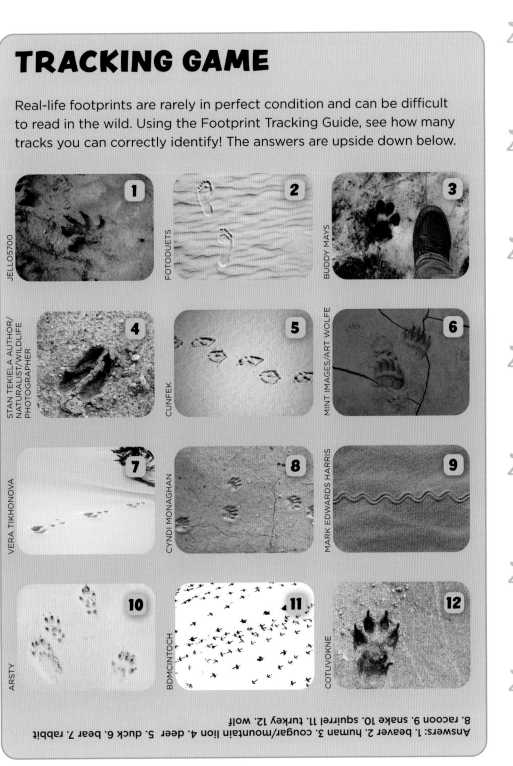

1 — JELLO5700
2 — FOTODUETS
3 — BUDDY MAYS
4 — STAN TEKIELA AUTHOR/NATURALIST/WILDLIFE PHOTOGRAPHER
5 — CUNFEK
6 — MINT IMAGES/ART WOLFE
7 — VERA TIKHONOVA
8 — CYNDI MONAGHAN
9 — MARK EDWARDS HARRIS
10 — ARSTY
11 — BDMCINTOCH
12 — COTUVOKNE

Answers: 1. beaver 2. human 3. cougar/mountain lion 4. deer 5. duck 6. bear 7. rabbit 8. racoon 9. snake 10. squirrel 11. turkey 12. wolf

ARE BITTEN BY A SMALL MAMMAL

Get away from the animal. Stop blood loss with direct pressure on the wound and elevation of the wound above the level of your heart. Wash the wound thoroughly with soap and water.

If the animal is infected with a disease, the bite may transmit the disease to you. But immediate cleaning of the wound will reduce the chances of transmission. After cleaning, gently dry the wound with sterile gauze or a clean, soft cloth. Cover it with a sterile dressing (from your first aid kit) or a clean, dry cloth.

If adults with you don't know you were bitten, tell them right away. They will want to find a doctor for you. The doctor will want to know when you were bitten, the geographical location of the attack, and the species of animal that bit you. A doctor will know best if anything else needs to be done for you.

MARK NEWMAN

Fun Fact: Shadow Wolf Trackers

In southern Arizona, along the rugged Mexico–United States desert border, there is an elite Native American tactical patrol unit called the Shadow Wolves. Using both ancient Native American tracking skills and modern technology, they serve as a critical part of the United States Homeland Security Department.

The Shadow Wolves use their advanced tracking skills to monitor the movement of smugglers on more than 2.8 million acres of the Tohono O'odham Nation. Between 2010 and 2020, they prevented more than 117,264 pounds of drugs from crossing the border!

KATHLEEN REEDER WILDLIFE PHOTOGRAPHY

ENCOUNTER A PORCUPINE

Don't mess with it. Move well away. Porcupines almost never bite. They do, however, carry an average of 30,000 quills. And while they cannot "shoot" the quills, the quills will embed easily in your body if you touch them. Each quill is barbed, and movement of your body causes an embedded quill to work in deeper. And the core of each quill is spongy, allowing it to absorb body moisture and swell. As a quill swells, the barbs expand, and getting it out becomes more difficult.

If you get stuck by porcupine quills, remove them as soon as possible. Take hold of each quill as close to your skin as you can get and pull it straight and gently out. Don't jerk or twist the quill. A pair of pliers or strong tweezers will help. This hurts, but there is no better way to extract the quills. Do not bother cutting off the top of the quill. The quill will not collapse, and extraction won't be easier. Fortunately, infection seldom results from embedded quills.

ENCOUNTER A SKUNK

Move well away. A skunk's spray comes from a sac in the rear end. To spray, the skunk turns its hindquarters toward a threat, lifts its tail, and fires. It can be accurate to at least 13 feet. A skunk can spray when lifted by its tail, and a skunk will bite if threatened. If skunk spray gets in your eyes, flush them with a flood of clean water. Your eyes may hurt for a while, but the pain will go away. The bad smell of skunk spray will not hurt you, but it can be a very long time before the stink goes away. So, yes, move well away from a skunk.

TOM BRAKEFIELD

ARE BOTHERED BY MICE

The main thing is not to give rodents a reason to bother you. Like all wild creatures, they are attracted to the possibility of a meal. Camp cleanly: Avoid dropping food scraps on the ground. Keep all food out of your tent. Keep all garbage in a bag. Clean your outdoor kitchen as soon as a meal is finished. After eating, hang your leftovers and garbage off the ground and away from the trunks of trees.

AMITH NAG PHOTOGRAPHY

FIND A DEAD ANIMAL

Don't touch it. The fur and feathers of dead animals can be hiding germs that make people sick. Fur, especially, may harbor insects, primarily fleas, whose bites may pass disease-causing germs to you. Plague, for instance, is transmitted by the bites of infected fleas. If you did contact a dead animal, maybe by accident, wash your hands soon. And wash them well. If the dead animal has been partially consumed by a predator, move away quickly, but do not run. The predator will almost always be returning, if it isn't already nearby.

FABA-PHOTOGRAPHY

HIKE IN RATTLESNAKE COUNTRY

Avoid stepping where you don't have a clear view of your path. Don't stick your hands into places that you can't check with your eyes first. If you gather firewood, do so while there is plenty of light. Keep your tent zipped shut.

If you hear the buzz of a rattler, freeze, then find the snake with your eyes without moving your head. Wait for it to relax the strike position, then back away slowly. If a snake comes toward you, it is almost always a snake that's not sure where you are. Turn and walk away quickly. If you can't find the snake with your eyes, slowly backtrack. If you see a snake, do not approach it. Never try to capture a snake. If you must pass near a rattlesnake, stay well outside of its strike range, a distance of one-half or, at most, two-thirds the snake's length.

GET BITTEN BY A VENOMOUS SNAKE

Do your best to stay calm. It is unusual to die from a snakebite from a species that inhabits the United States. Remove rings, watches, or anything else near the bite site that might reduce circulation if swelling occurs. Wash the wound. Splint a bitten arm or leg (see Break an Arm or Leg) and keep the arm or leg at approximately the same level as your heart. Keep yourself warm. Keep yourself well hydrated unless vomiting becomes a problem. Do not cut and suck. Do not apply cold to the bite site. Do not use a tourniquet.

An adult with you should go for help or send someone for help. Walking around is not at all recommended. But if someone with you can carry you, that would be OK.

STEPHEN GORMAN

Water moccasin

SURVIVAL TIP: CELL PHONES AS A SURVIVAL TOOL

Did you know that cell phones have functions that can be used as a survival tool?

Call for help! If you have a signal, you can call for help. Get on the phone and call 911, just like you would do at home!

Find your location! Map apps on your phone can help determine your location. There are amazing trail and compass apps specifically designed to navigate the backcountry. Remember to download these apps *before* you leave on your trip!

Signal mirror! In the same way you can use a mirror to reflect and direct light from the sun to another object as a way to signal for help, you can do the same thing with the glass of your phone.

Binoculars! On many phones it's possible to use your camera to zoom in on an area you want to take a closer look at. You can also take a photo of that area and then zoom in on the photo.

Google it! Need some help with a first aid technique or making a shelter? If you've got a signal, google it!

Portable library! *Before* you leave, you can download survival books onto your phone as a reference when you need them.

Flashlight! Your screen or the flashlight can serve as source of light if you forgot your flashlight.

Note: It's important to remember that cell phones break, their batteries can die, and it's easy to lose a signal in the backcountry. While a cell phone can be helpful in a survival situation, they are never a substitute for the 11 essentials!

GPOINTSTUDI

GET BITTEN BY A SPIDER

Stay calm. Most spider bites are harmless. Since many bites cause little or no pain, you may even be unaware you were bitten. In the United States, there are three dangerous spiders: black widows, brown recluses, and hobo spiders. Their bites, over time, may produce intense pain and/or a skin ulcer.

If a spider bite starts to hurt, apply cold for the pain. Cold also reduces circulation, which slows down the spread of spider venom. If it's in your first aid kit, apply an antiseptic. Also, if the pain becomes intense, fever and weakness develop, and/or a skin ulcer appears at the bite site, you need to see a doctor as soon as possible. Recovery from serious spider bites in the United States is almost always assured with proper medical care.

Hobo spider

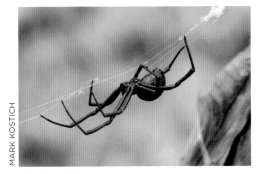

Black widow

Mediterranean recluse spider

GET BITTEN BY A TICK

Ticks may be carrying some nasty germs, but they do not pass germs until they embed and feed, so remove embedded ticks as soon as possible. Use tweezers to grasp the tick where it has buried its head in your skin. If you have a choice, use tweezers that are sharply pointed. They squeeze the tick less. Keep the tweezers perpendicular to the long axis of the tick's short body to prevent squeezing it (see photo).

If you don't have tweezers, grasp the tick as gently as possible with your fingers. Pull it out slowly without yanking or twisting. After the tick is out, wash the area with alcohol, antibiotic ointment, or soap and

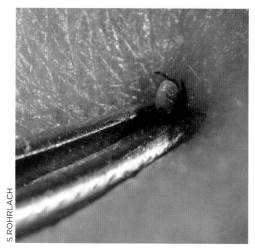
Grasp the tick where it has buried its head.

water—and wash your hands if you touched the tick. If possible, save the tick in a closed container for lab testing in case you get sick.

SURVIVAL TIP: GET AND STAY FIT

Spending most of your days sitting in your classroom or playing video games is not good preparation for outdoor adventures. Find a sport or exercise you enjoy and make yourself stronger! That effort will pay off big-time.

FATCAMERA

GET STUNG BY A SCORPION

Stay calm and still. Panic and activity speed up the spread of a scorpion's venom. Use an ice pack or cold running water to cool the site of the sting as soon as possible. Use a wet compress if nothing else is available. Cold will reduce the pain, which is typically no worse than a bad bee sting. The only North American scorpion to cause serious problems in humans is *Centruroides* (bark scorpion). They live nowhere but in the extreme Southwest.

A *Centruroides* sting may cause heavy sweating, difficulty swallowing, blurred vision, incontinence (loss of bowel control), jerky muscular reflexes, and trouble breathing. These serious reactions are cause for a quick trip to a medical facility. Drugs to reverse the bad effects are generally available in areas where dangerous scorpions live.

JASONONDREICKA

Bark scorpion

Bee

ENCOUNTER BEES OR WASPS

Stay calm and back away slowly. Bees and wasps are agitated by rapid movements, especially swatting motions.

If you're stung, the barbed stinger left in you by a honeybee should be removed as soon as possible. The method of removal doesn't matter—scrape it out, scratch it out, pull it out. When the barbed stinger rips out of a honeybee, it includes the venom sac, which will continue to pump venom for up to 20 minutes. Bumblebees (which are fatter and generally less aggressive than honeybees) and wasps may sting, but they do not leave their stingers behind.

In all cases of being stung, an application of something cold will reduce the pain. If available, wipe the sting site with an antiseptic (if it's in your first aid kit). If you know you are allergic to bee or wasp stings, always carry a bee sting kit.

Wasp

ARE BOTHERED BY BITING INSECTS

Wear clothing thick enough or tightly woven enough to prevent penetration of the insect's biting apparatus. Wear long sleeves and long pants to reduce the amount of skin that insects have access to. Some insects, especially mosquitoes, seem to be partial to dark colors, particularly blue, so wear light-colored clothing (khaki, for example). Wear a head net. Apply permethrin, a safe insecticide, to clothing (but do not use if you have cats, as it is toxic to them). Apply an insect repellent containing DEET or lemon eucalyptus oil to exposed skin. Sleep under mosquito netting or inside a tent with mosquito netting. Avoid exposure during prime biting time, usually dawn and dusk.

STEPHEN GORMAN AND ELI BURAKIAN

Chemicals that keep the bugs off

Smoky fires, when acceptable and possible, deter many insects. Avoid insect habitat: standing water, dense vegetation, and areas that you hear people say are thick with biting insects.

ONFOKUS

Bug netting

DORIOCONNEL

GET BITTEN BY A MOSQUITO

What is more common than a mosquito bite? Topical (stuff that you put on your skin) anti-itch products will work to reduce the itching. So will over-the-counter oral antihistamines (if your parents have approved them). Products that contain benzocaine will reduce pain. Steroid creams have little or no effect. Wash and then keep an eye on mosquito bites that have been scratched open. Watch for signs of infection: increasing redness and swelling, increasing pain, red streaks appearing just beneath the skin. Infected bites should be treated by a doctor.

GET STUNG BY A JELLYFISH

If you touch the tentacles of a jelly-fish, tiny barbed stingers often stick in you. They cause pain, and the pain has caused some people to panic and drown. So get yourself out of the water immediately. Once safely on shore, rinse the irritated area with large amounts of sea water. Vinegar, if some is around, is even better. But don't rinse with fresh water. It might make the stinging worse. Lift off any clinging tentacles, but do so without touching the tentacles with a naked hand. Someone wearing gloves can remove tentacles. Tweezers work, too. If water can be heated, a bath of hot water sometimes eases the pain. Don't rub the irritated part of your body. And don't try to scrape off the stingers. If the pain is really bother-ing you, you want to consult a doc-tor. If you have a serious reaction—especially difficulty breathing—find a doctor as soon as possible.

DOBRILA VIGNJEVIC

SURVIVAL TIP: FIRST AID

A first aid kit is one of the 11 essentials you should bring on your outdoor adventures. First aid kits can be purchased from a store with preselected items inside. Most kits probably won't have everything you need on this list so you will likely have to buy a few extra items or build one yourself from scratch.

Here's a list of important items you should find in a hiking first aid kit:

Helpful tools:
    Tweezers
    Scissors
    First aid manual
    Sewing needle
    Safety pin
    Water purification tablets
    Nail clippers
In case you get sick:
    EpiPen, if someone in your group has allergies to food or bee stings
    Pain relief and anti-inflammatory medicine for pain or to reduce
        inflammation
    Oral antihistamine for allergic reaction
    Antidiarrheal in case you get sick

ARISARA_TONGDONNOI

Hydrocortisone anti-itch cream
Laxative in case you can't "go"
Electrolyte powder
Anti-itch cream
In case you get hurt:
Hand sanitizer
Elastic bandage for sprains
Bandages for cuts in different sizes
Antibiotic ointment to prevent an infection in a cut
Antiseptic/alcohol wipes to clean wounds
Medical gloves, to avoid contamination
Butterfly wound closures, like Steri-Strips
4x4 dressing pads
Rolled gauze for larger cuts
Medical tape to help secure gauze or bandages
Moleskin for blisters
Sunburn relief like aloe vera gel

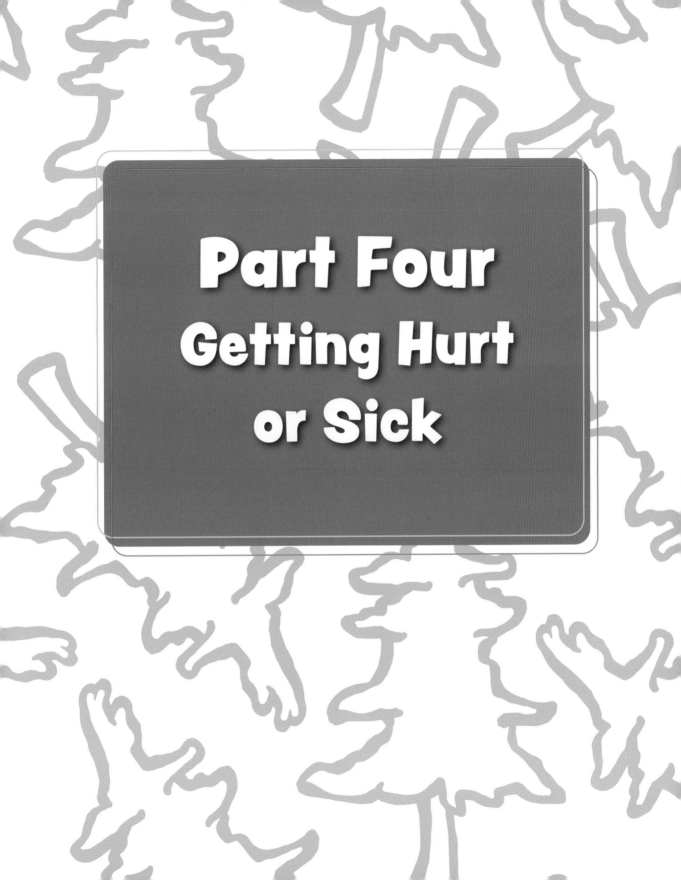

Part Four
Getting Hurt or Sick

WHAT IF YOU . . .

GET FROSTBITE

There are levels of frostbite. When it occurs, a part of your body has gotten too cold. If your skin is pale and numb but not hard, warm it immediately with skin-to-skin contact. You can, for instance, put your cold hand against someone's warm abdomen. Don't rub the skin or put it near a source of high heat. Skin that returns to normal appearance is probably OK, but if blisters form, find a physician. If you can't walk, send someone for help.

Hard frostbite is best treated by warming in water of approximately 104–108°F, about the same temperature as water in a hot tub. Soft, clean material should be placed between thawed digits (fingers and toes), but contact with anything else should be avoided. Pain is often intense. Find a doctor as soon as you can. If you can't get warm water, it's almost always best to keep moving until you can.

Once hard frostbite thaws, especially on your feet, you may be unable to walk. If there's ibuprofen in the first aid kit, and someone responsible says it's OK, take the recommended dose for your age. In all cases, stay well hydrated and do everything possible to prevent refreezing.

STEPHEN GORMAN AND ELI BURAKIAN

Warm cold feet against someone's stomach.

STEPHEN GORMAN AND ELI BURAKIAN

Treat cold hands in warm water.

GET HEAT EXHAUSTION

When it's hot and you get super tired, you may have heat exhaustion. Stop. Rest in the shade. Sip cool water or a sports drink until you feel OK. If you drink plain water, a salty snack may be beneficial. The fatigue, headache, and nausea of heat exhaustion are indications of internal water depletion. Once you've rested and rehydrated, you'll be fine, and you can continue on your way.

MIXETTO

GET HEATSTROKE

Heatstroke is happening on a hot day when your internal temperature starts to rise—like when you have a fever. You need to cool off immediately. Heatstroke can be a life-threatening emergency. If you suffer from an altered level of consciousness and have red, hot skin, your core temperature has already risen to dangerous levels. You need to be in the shade and stripped down to thin, cotton layers or nothing. Water should be poured over you repeatedly. If water is in short supply, the cooling efforts should be concentrated on your head. You need to be vigorously fanned. Massaging will help bring cooler surface blood to your overheated core. Ice packs should be placed on your neck, armpits, and groin, if possible. Even if you seem to return to normal, you should see a doctor as soon as possible. Complications from heatstroke are common.

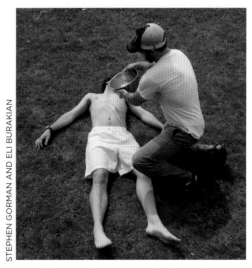

STEPHEN GORMAN AND ELI BURAKIAN

Applying cold water is the fastest way to cool a person down.

Altitude Sickness

Altitude sickness is a common problem when hikers reach 8,000 feet above sea level or higher. When people climb too high, too quickly, the sudden reduction in air pressure and oxygen levels can cause their bodies to not get enough oxygen. This lack of oxygen can cause headaches, nausea, loss of appetite, vomiting, shortness of breath, sleep problems, and a lack of energy. In more severe cases, hikers may even require medical attention.

One of the best ways to prevent altitude sickness is to give your body time to "acclimate" or get used to the higher altitudes. Mount Everest is the highest mountain in the world, standing 29,029 feet tall. Climbers of Mount Everest are advised to rest for a day or two after every 2,000 feet they climb. This is to help their bodies acclimate.

If you think you or your hiking buddy might be suffering from altitude sickness, descend 1,500 to 3,000 feet together. If you don't feel better within a few hours, exit the trail and seek medical attention.

CHRISTIANNASCA

This climber brought a portable oxygen cylinder to avoid a medical emergency.

GET DIARRHEA

Dehydration (getting low on internal water) is the immediate threat with diarrhea. Mild diarrhea can be treated by sipping water, diluted fruit juice, or a sports drink. Persistent diarrhea (it just won't stop) requires a more aggressive replacement of electrolytes. You can make a rehydration solution by adding 1 teaspoon of salt and 8 teaspoons of sugar to 1 liter of water. Drink about a quarter (1 cup) of this solution every hour, along with all the plain water you can tolerate.

Rice, grains, bananas, and potatoes are OK to eat. Avoid fatty foods, dairy products, and drinks with caffeine. If the diarrhea is not under control in 24 to 72 hours or if you have blood in your stool and a fever, see a doctor. Ask your parents about including an antidiarrheal med in your first aid kit.

ARE POISONED BY SOMETHING YOU ATE

After reading the first section of this book, you know you can go a very long time without eating (see Run Out of Food). And the safest thing to do is *never* eat anything unless you are totally sure it's good as human

LUCENTIUS

RUBBERBALL/MIKE KEMP

food. But if someone swallows anything that might be poisonous, drinking as much water as possible can be helpful. The water dilutes the poison. Don't try to make the person vomit. It's just not safe. In case something poisonous was swallowed, the best action is to head for a doctor. The doctor will want to know what was eaten, when, and how much.

COME IN CONTACT WITH POISON IVY

Leaves of three? Let it be! But if you think you touched poison ivy or poison oak, wash as soon as possible. Cold water, lots of it, inactivates the toxin. Avoid hot water. If more than 3 minutes have passed since con-

CONNERS

Poison ivy exposure

Poison ivy

tact, wash with cold water and soap. Wash five or six times with rinses in between.

When you wash your hands, be sure to clean under your fingernails.

Also, wash any gear or clothes that may be contaminated. Clothing may hold the oil, protecting your skin at first, but the oil will remain active for a long, long time, returning to haunt you if you don't wash clothing thoroughly.

If an itchy rash develops anyway, check with a doctor about medications that can help.

If you touch poison ivy, wash immediately.

GET STUCK WITH CACTUS SPINES

With tweezers or small pliers, pull the spines straight and gently out. You may be able to improvise tweezers by splitting a small stick and squeezing the spines between the halves. If it's available, smear glue or rubber cement on small spines. Then press a piece of gauze into the glue while it's still moist. After it dries, peel off the gauze with the layer of glue or cement. A very high percentage of the spines will come out this way. Infections from cactus spines are uncommon.

The spines of the cholla (jumping) cactus often come off the plant in pieces. You can usually pry out an embedded cholla with a comb. Taking a firm grip on the cholla with pliers or tongs and pulling also works. This might hurt.

Cholla or jumping cactus

SURVIVAL TIP: SITUATIONAL AWARENESS

Most people are afraid of sharks, but did you know more people die from taking a selfie than from shark attacks every year? This unfortunate fact reminds us of how important it is to pay attention to changing conditions when we are outside. This is called situational awareness.

Three components of situational awareness are:

Observe: Few things change in the comfort of your home, but the wilderness is always changing. Outdoorsmen and -women must attune their senses to these frequent changes in the environment and be prepared for anything.

Using your senses is critical to situational awareness. Is there a storm forming? Do your eyes recognize that the clouds are building up and getting darker? Do your ears hear the changes in the wind or the distant sound of thunder? Can you feel the sticky humidity on your skin or smell the distant rain?

Comprehend: What do those changes in your environment mean? If you think it will storm soon, what are your safety options? Should you hunker down and set up camp early or cut your hike short and head to the car? These decisions are dynamic and will vary as your personal situation varies.

Act: This is where you take action based upon your understanding of the danger. If you think a storm is coming, act in a way to avoid a survival situation.

GET A SPLINTER

Get it out or it could become infected. If the end is visible, grasp it with tweezers and pull it gently out. If the end is buried, see if you can push with your fingers until the splinter appears in the opening of the wound. Then grasp the splinter and pull it out. With deeply buried splinters, it is usually best to find a doctor who can help. You don't need to rush, but remember, embedded splinters can become infected.

GET SOMETHING LOOSE IN YOUR EYE

Do not rub your eye. The problem is seldom serious, but rubbing can make it so. Things such as dirt, hair, or insects in the eye can cause enormous discomfort, and the stuff should be removed. If you relax and allow your eye to naturally fill with tears, they will often wash the eye clean. You can safely speed up the process by lying on your back and

SUTTHIWAT SRIKHRUEADAM

PHEELINGS MEDIA

out. Please don't try to pick something out of your eye. Wash it out.

GET A CUT

Cuts are often not very serious, but if you are bleeding, apply pressure with your hand directly to the cut and elevate the site higher than your heart. When the bleeding has stopped, do what you can to prevent infection. Clean the wound. Irrigation works best. You can use a water bottle with a squirt top or punch a pinhole in a plastic bag. Irrigate with at least one quart of water.

After cleaning, if the width of the wound is less than half an inch, pull the edges back to their original position with thin strips of tape. Cover

pouring a gentle stream of clean water on the bridge of your nose. Blink rapidly, and the offending object or objects should soon float

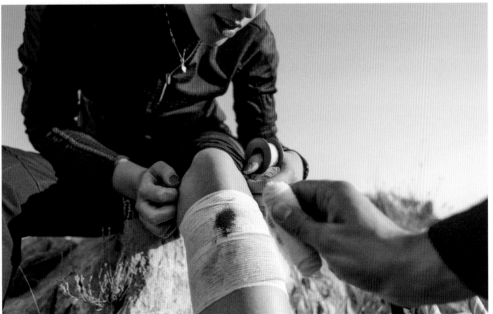

FLUXFACTORY

the closed cut with antibiotic ointment, sterile gauze, and tape. If the width of the wound is a half inch or more, cover it with sterile gauze and tape and see a doctor.

CATCH YOURSELF ON FIRE

Stop, drop, and roll on the ground. You are smothering the flames. Immediately remove any smoldering clothing, unless synthetics have melted and stuck to the burn site. Leave melted clothing in place. Remove anything—rings, bracelets, watches—that might cut off circulation if swelling occurs. Immediately cool burned skin with water: your arm in a stream, hand in a pot of water, arm wrapped in wet cotton, and so on. Keep cooling the wound until the pain is at least temporarily gone. Yes, it will hurt. Stay well hydrated. If blisters form and/or you see alarmingly pale or charred skin, cover the burn site with a clean, dry cloth and get to a doctor.

GET SUNBURNED

Not getting sunburned is important, and that's why sun protection is a part of the 11 essentials (see Pack the 11 Essentials). But if you do get sunburned, avoid further exposure to direct sunlight. As soon as possible, soak burned skin in cool water or apply a wet cotton cloth, such as a wet T-shirt. After cooling, apply a moisturizing lotion or cream that includes aloe. Stay well hydrated. If blisters develop, see a doctor.

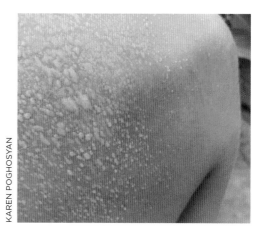

KAREN POGHOSYAN

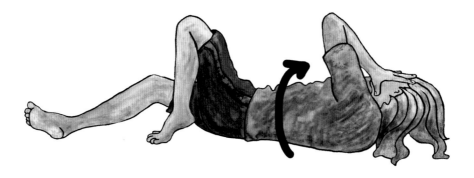

GET A BLISTER

If the bubble (usually on your heel) is intact, not broken open, wash it thoroughly and gently. Sterilize the tip of a knife in a flame or wipe it with alcohol. Have someone you trust carefully slice the blister open and let it drain until the fluid is gone. After draining, reduce the friction on the blister as much as possible. A simple and proven technique involves creating a moleskin or mole foam "doughnut" to surround the blister site, then filling the hole with a glob of gooey ointment—sort of a jelly-filled doughnut. Any ointment will work. A second patch of moleskin or a strip of tape over the filled doughnut will keep the ointment in place.

TWIST YOUR ANKLE

It's best to not walk on a twisted ankle, but, well, sometimes you have to because you're way out there. When you first hurt your ankle, stop using it. Take a look at it. A lot of swelling and discoloration means a lot of damage. Rest for about 5 minutes, then test the ankle gently. If you can walk on it, you can keep using it to walk out. But first, cool the ankle with ice, cold water, or snow, or even by wrapping it in wet cotton.

To treat a twisted ankle, compress it with an elastic wrap, and keep it elevated higher than your heart.

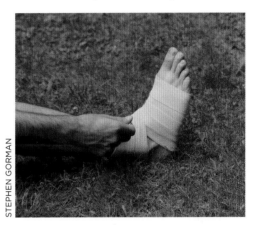

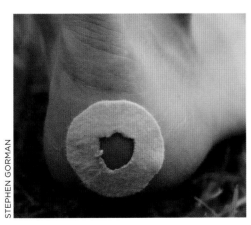

Moleskin cut around the blister

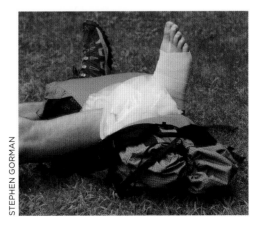

(An elastic wrap is a great addition to your first aid kit.) Keep up the rest, ice, compression, and elevation (RICE) for no more than 30 minutes. Then allow adequate time for the ankle to warm back up, usually about 15 minutes. You can repeat RICE as often as necessary.

If you can't walk on it, the ankle will need a splint (see Break an Arm or Leg). You'll need a doctor.

BREAK AN ARM OR LEG

You may not know for sure if it's broken, but if you don't want to use your injured arm or leg, it's almost always best to think it's broken.

Splint it. A good splint starts with a lot of padding. Wrap the injured extremity in extra clothing or anything soft. Attach something rigid outside the padding. The rigid support should immobilize the joints above and below a mid-bone break, as well as the bones above and below a break near a joint. A broken ankle, for instance, should be splinted to immobilize the foot and lower leg. Attach the rigid support with whatever is available: elastic wraps, strips

SRDJANNS74

STEPHEN GORMAN AND ELI BURAKIAN

Hiker applies a splint (rigid support) under his broken arm.

of torn T-shirt, bandannas, and so on. Check to make sure your splint does not interfere with normal circulation. With a splinted arm, you can walk out. With a splinted leg, you'll need someone to go for help.

GET A NOSEBLEED

Lean forward slightly to prevent blood from running down your throat. Pinch the fleshy part of your nostrils closed. This is using direct pressure to stop the bleeding. Keep pinching until the bleeding stops, usually only a few minutes. Restrain yourself from nose picking for a couple of days. If you're susceptible to nosebleeds, an application of ointment to the inside of your nose once or twice a day will keep your nasal membranes moist and prevent some nosebleeds. The same stuff you use on dry lips will work. Apply gently.

SOLSTOCK

LEARN FIRST AID AND CPR!

First aid and CPR (cardiopulmonary resuscitation) are important skills to have because they can save a life! Did you know that you don't have to be an adult to learn first aid and CPR? Kids can learn these skills too!

Research shows that kids as young as 6 years old can start learning first aid and kids as young as 9 can learn the basics of CPR! The American Heart Association, the American Red Cross, and many scouting organizations offer first aid and CPR training programs specifically designed for children. Like all things new, learning these skills will require practice and repeated training.

First aid and CPR aren't just important for the backcountry. In 2016, a 13-year-old boy from Arizona named Isaac learned CPR in the Boy Scouts and saved his baseball coach when he had a heart attack. Isaac knew to call 911 and administered CPR, which saved his coach's life!

GAHSOON

Let an adult know that you are interested in taking these classes and one day you might save another person's life too!

Part Five
A Few
Other Things

HAVE TO GO TO THE BATHROOM

When you need to go, well, you need to go. But do it appropriately if you have a choice. Dig a cat hole, a hole in the ground 6 to 8 inches deep and at least 200 feet (about 70 big steps) from water, camp, and trails. If you choose to use toilet paper, pack it out in a plastic bag or burn it in your campfire. You may choose to wipe with leaves, grass, or snow and deposit the wiping material in the cat hole. When finished, fill and hide the cat hole.

Urinate well away from camps and trails, and on rocks or bare ground rather than on vegetation. Where water is plentiful, dilute the urine by rinsing the site. You may also urinate into large bodies of water: rivers and lakes.

STEPHEN GORMAN

An outhouse

SURVIVAL TIP: WIDOW-MAKERS

"Widow-maker" is a term that refers to dead or broken trees and their limbs that can fall and hurt you. When deciding where to camp or take a break, be sure to look up and check that the trees and branches above you are healthy and strong.

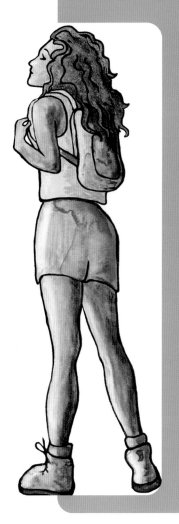

JACKY PARKER PHOTOGRAPHY

Widow-maker

BREAK A SHOESTRING

You can almost always continue with the longest piece of the broken shoestring. Re-lace the shoe or boot, skipping the eyelets near your toes. In a standard hiking boot, your foot is held in place primarily by the laces from where your ankle bends to the top of the boot. Any shoe will stay in place even if the first few eyelets nearest the toe are skipped. If an entire shoestring is lost, cut the other one in half. You may, of course, find cord in your gear to use as an improvised shoestring. Or you can cut a replacement shoestring off one of the lines of your tent.

IMGORTHAND

BREAK OR LOSE YOUR SUNGLASSES

Since the earpiece usually breaks, you can often tape the broken piece back in place. If the glasses break at the nosepiece, you may be able to mend that with tape too. A small safety pin may be used to replace a lost pin from where an earpiece attaches to the frame. Tape and a safety pin are excellent choices for things to put in your first aid kit.

If your sunglasses are unfixable or lost, there are several ways to improvise a pair. Cut a piece of cardboard—such as a food package—to fit over your eyes, and cut two slices or holes in the cardboard to see through. Or tie a bandanna over your eyes after cutting two small holes to see through. Or cut two lengths of duct tape and stick them together, sticky sides in, then cut two slices or holes to see through. You can use string to hold the improvised sunglasses in place, or you can use tape long enough to tie behind your head.

АНАТОЛИЙ ТУШЕНЦОВ

VIROJT CHANGYENCHAM

USE TREKKING POLES

It's like using ski poles except, well, you're not skiing. Many hikers do not use them, but those who do love them. Since you want to come back from out there, trekking poles can be very helpful.

They improve your balance, so there's less chance you'll fall and get hurt. With better balance, you have more energy for hiking. If you're wearing a pack, poles take some of the strain off your shoulders. They can be a part of a shelter, such as propping up both ends of a tarp.

Or one pole in the middle can hold up a tarp. Raise them above your head if you want to look bigger and scarier to wildlife.

To know you have your poles at the best length, hold onto the grip of the pole and hold your bent elbow close to your side. The tip of your pole should just reach the ground.